Warren Benson

THREE DOZEN DELIGHTS, DEDICATIONS, APHORISMS, ALLELUIAS, AMENS, EXHORTATIONS, AND BENEDICTIONS

for
WORSHIP, CANONICAL EXERCISE,
CEREMONY, AND ENJOYMENT

to be sung by
MIXED CHORUS A CAPPELLA
with
occasional keyboard accompaniment

ISBN 978-1-5400-1523-5

 |

www.ebmarks.com
www.halleonard.com

* accompaniment required

1. Hear How the Birds

Text: Alexander Pope

Warren Benson

2. Joy is with us!

3. Vocalise

4. I Like the Laughter

Victor Hugo

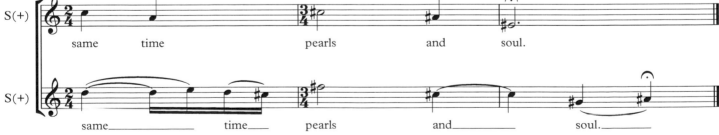

Blank for Page Turns

5. Love Can Sun

Friedrick Schiller

6. I Want To Do Right

Riff Ostinati

Double Choir canon or div. choir:

1) All sections, in turn: SATB, sing their riff, <u>soli</u> (in rhythm):

2) Then, in the same order, by adding sections on one at a time:

3) Then, in the same order, adding canonic choir one section at a time at (X):

4) Repeat full canon 4 times.

5) Finally, reverse the process, omitting sections one at a time, in order,
   until 6) only the canonic soprano line is left to end the piece with
   repeated verses dying away to silence.

7) It should "swing".

pp   (4x)

```
S → A → T → B → ⎧ S   S   S   S   S   S   S │ S   S   S   S │
                ⎪     A   A   A   A   A   A │ A   A   A   A │ A
                ⎨         T   T   T   T   T │ T   T   T   T │ T   T
                ⎪             B   B   B   B │ B   B   B   B │ B   B   B
                ⎩                 S   S   S │ S   S   S   S │ S   S   S   S   S   S   S
                                      A   A │ A   A   A   A │ A   A   A   A   A   A
                                          T │ T   T   T   T │ T   T   T   T   T
                                            │ B   B   B   B │ B   B   B   B
```

                                             (4x)

                    f ══════════════════════════════ *pp*

7. Love is Precisely
Canonic Song

Honoré de Balzac

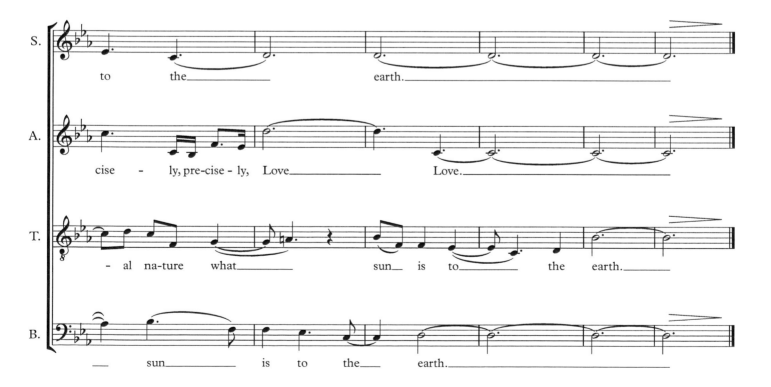

8. Love Is The Spirit

James Vila Blake
(from the covenant adopted by the
Church of All Souls, Evanston, Illinois, 1894.)

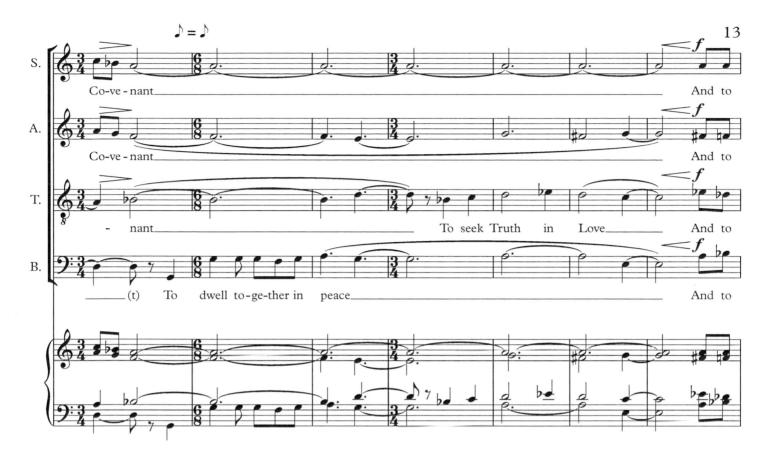

9. It is Love

St. Augustine (adapted)

10. A Friend Is

Table Canon

Traditional

Table Canon

10. A Friend Is

16

11. Ev'ry Simple Reaching

Blank for Page Turns

12. It Is Better
Double Canon

Bishop Cumberland

* May be done with 3 repeats, voices entering as follows:
  1. S.T. all the way through
  2. ST+AB (use 1st ending, until 4th time)
  3. ST+AB+Solo #1 (repeating from 2nd ending cue)
  4. ST+AB+#1+Solo #2 - to 2nd ending conclusion)

If done 4 times, begin **p** and increase dynamic level on successive repeats.

(Normal response performance: ST+AB 1st time, +2 Solos 2nd time.)

(Instruments may be substituted for soprano soloists.)

13. A Loving Heart

2-part Canon

Charles Dickens

* for two-part use top and bottom lines, last three measures.

14. Amor Vincit Omnia
Double Canon in Inversion

Traditional

15. Children have more need

Joseph Joubert

♩ = 116

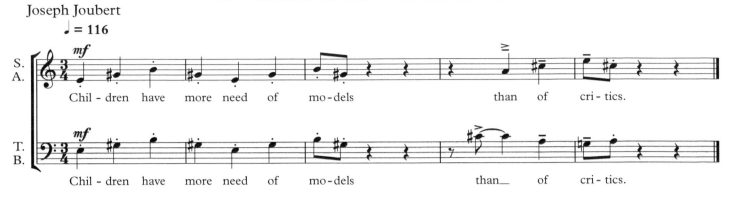

Chil - dren have more need of mo - dels than of cri - tics.

Chil - dren have more need of mo - dels than of cri - tics.

16. Alleluia
Table Canon

17. Gloria

18. Let Us Join Together
Four-Part Round

1. Tenor *
2. Alto
3. Soprano
4. Bass

Let us join to - ge - ther in a song of joy___ Al - le,___

___ Al - le,___ Al - le,___ Al - le,___ Al - le -

lu - ia, lu - ia, lu - ia, lu - ia,

Al - le - lu - ia, Al - le - lu - ia,___

___ Al - le - lu - ia,___ Al - le - lu - ia,___

le - lu - ia,___ Al - le - lu - ia,___ Let us
(Al - le)

* May repeat only last 4 lines, or all; or all, then first 4 fading away with all voices continuing.

19. Laude
Two-Voice Canon in Inversion

20. Whisper Hosanna

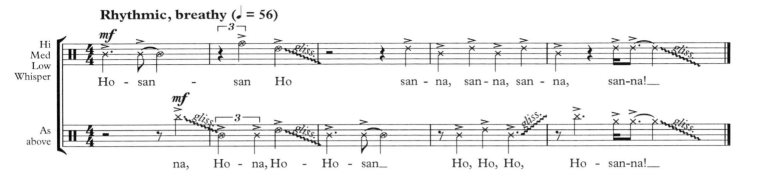

Rhythmic, breathy (♩ = 56)

Ho - san - - san Ho   san - na, san - na, san - na,   san-na!__

na, Ho - na, Ho - Ho - san__   Ho, Ho, Ho,   Ho - san-na!__

21. Alleluia, sing we.

22. Alleluia!

23. Threefold Amen

Smoothly ♩ = 72

24. Fourfold Amen

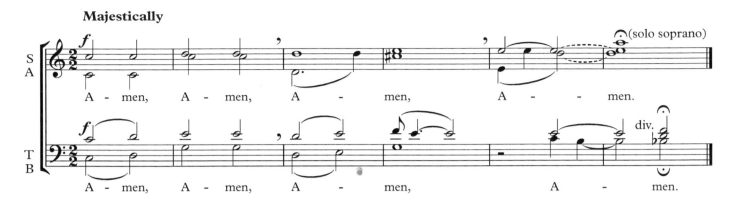

Majestically

A - men, A - men, A - men, A - - men.

A - men, A - men, A - men, A - - men.

25. Amen: Forty-Nine Fold

26. Cast Thy Bread

Biblical

27. Take Time
Unison and Keyboard

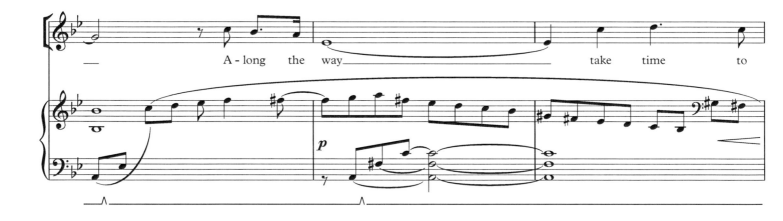

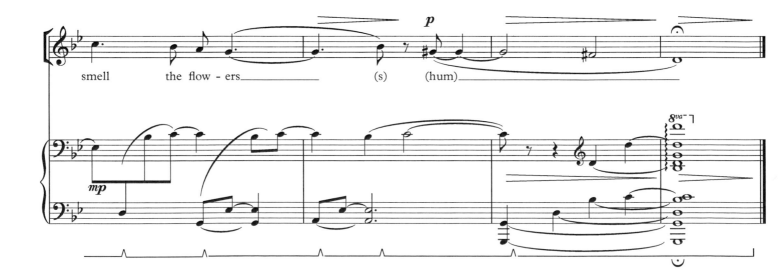

28. Grateful Be
4-part Canon

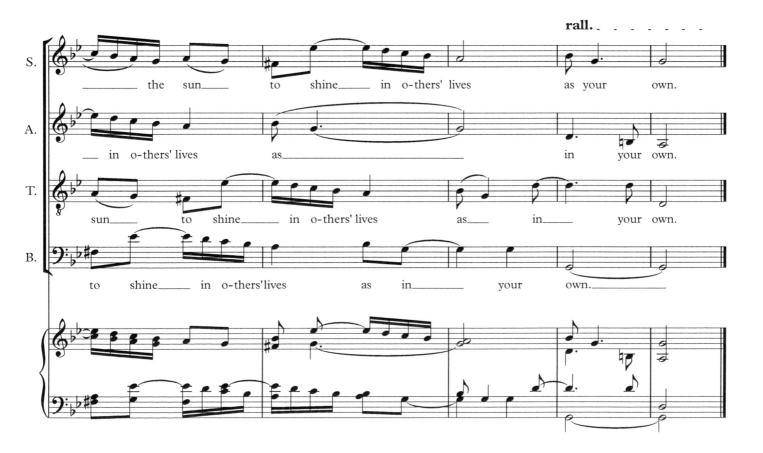

29. We Who Would Pass
2-part Canon

Joseph Addison (revised)

30. Love One Another

Brightly (♩. = 76)

31. Give Me the Ready Hand

Giuseppe Garibaldi

A. Give me the read - y hand ra - ther than the read - y tongue.

B. Give me the__ read - y hand ra - ther than the read - y tongue.__

32. Reach Out
Double Canon

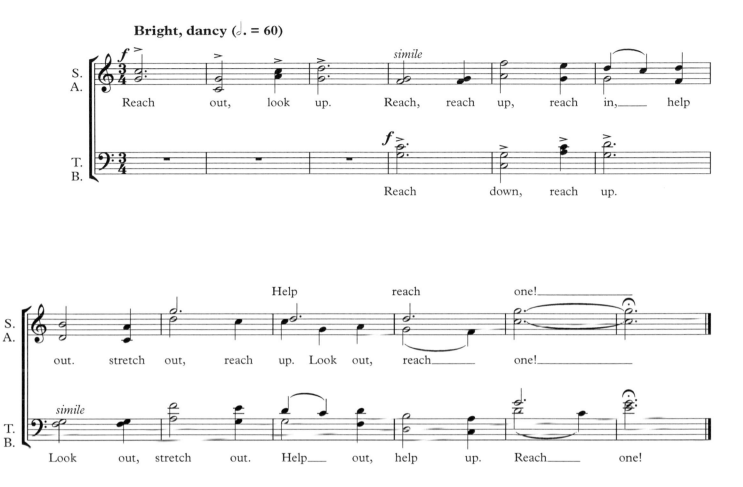

33. A Larger Circle
4-part ostinato

repeat at least once (each = :30)

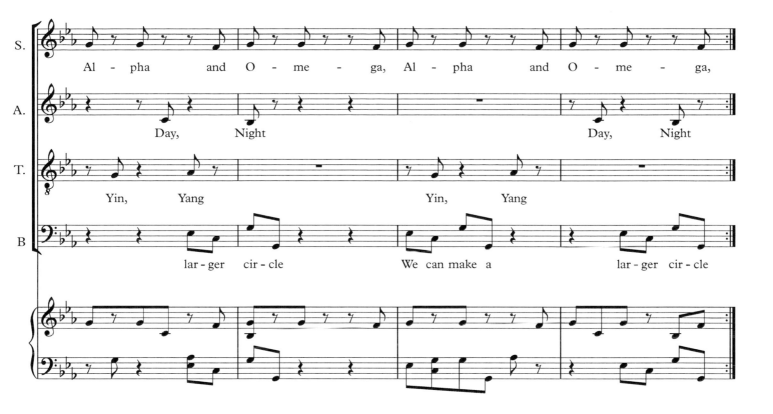

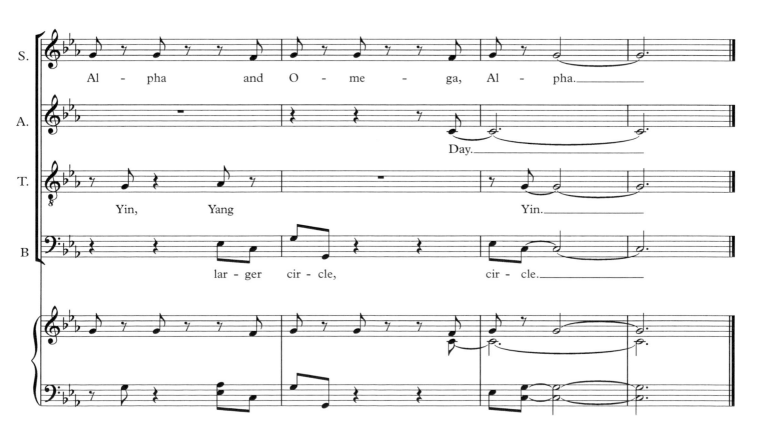

34. If You Wish

Seneca the Younger

35. Peace Be With You

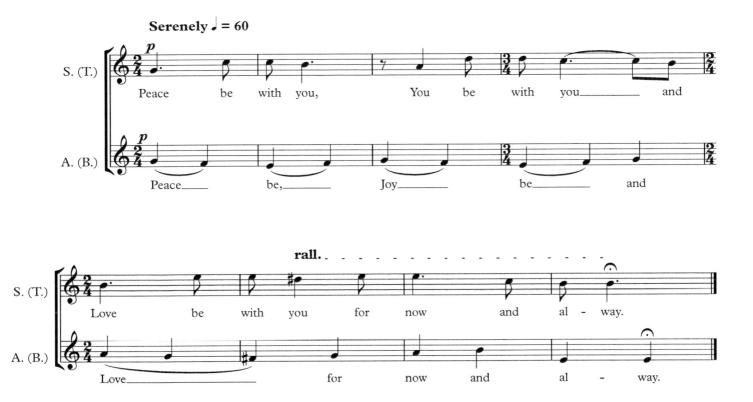

36. Shalom

37. Peace Be With Us

Ostinato

* 1. Soli 2. add all others, total 5 times, then to 6.

38. May the rains fall soft

47

39. Free-fold response

Having chosen the appropriate response text for the situation (*Amen*, *Dona nobis pacem*, *Shalom*, etc.), one person begins singing it very softly on a comfortable mid-range pitch.

The others gradually join in, on the same pitch (or octave), very softly, in random, individual rhythms. Sing for thirty seconds, all fading to silence.